Drama in the Garden

Drama in the Garden

Dorothy Loa McFadden

To Carol Greentree —
Who loves gardens
too. Affectionately
Dorothy Loa McFadden (Bruegge)

LITTLE OWL PRESS

Dorothy Loa McFadden, Publisher
2404 Loring Street, Box 288
San Diego, California
92109

Other garden books by Dorothy Loa McFadden:
Touring the Gardens of Europe, McKay Publishing, 1965, Library
   Guild Selection of American Garden Guild Book Club
Gardens of Europe, A Pictorial Tour, 1970, A.S. Barnes, Publisher
Oriental Gardens in America, 1976, Douglas West, Publisher
These books are out-of-print, but may be located by your librarian or
booksellers specializing in out-of-print editions.

COVER PHOTO: *GENERALIFE, ACEQUIA'S PATIO, SPAIN*
By James L. McFadden

ISBN 0-9634140-0-3
Library of Congress Catalog Card Number 92-097120
Printed in the United States of America

Contents

Foreword 7

Acknowledgments 11

Country Maps of the Twelve Gardens 15

Chapter 1, Melun, France .... Vaux-le-Vicomte
The Garden Party that Put the Host in Jail
(for the Rest of his Life) *19*

Chapter 2, Paris, France .... Bagatelle
When Marie-Antoinette Lost a Bet *27*

Chapter 3, Paris, France .... Roseraie
A Living History of the Rose *33*

Chapter 4, England .... Hampton Court
King Henry VIII and His Beasties *37*

Chapter 5, Lake District, England .... Levens Hall
Laughter in the Garden *43*

Chapter 6, Enniskerry, Ireland .... Powerscourt
The Gardener in the Wheelbarrow *49*

Chapter 7, Scotland .... Cawdor Castle
500 Year Old Legend Proven True Today *55*

Chapter 8, Germany .... Island of Mainau
A Great Gardener for Mankind *61*

Chapter 9, Hannover, Germany .... Herrenhausen
A Glorious Garden for the Arts *69*

Chapter 10, Austria .... Salzburg and Hellbrunn
Two Gardens for Three Mistresses *75*

Chapter 11 Granada, Spain .... The Alhambra
The Creation of a Wise Moorish Conqueror *81*

About the Author 89

Bibliography 93

The Gardens in Color 97

Foreword

The reader of this book will find that searching for the 'genesis' of ideas for each garden is a very gratifying and rewarding endeavor. If the ideas have lasted (probably more than seven generations) you will find the Creator's Hand at work. When I was younger, I felt that formal gardens were just power plays on the Creator's natural beauty. But as I matured, I realized that He wants to create *with* us.

Ideas should be judged by their longevity and the beautiful change they produce. In Grand Music and Gardens this change is generally in our feelings. The longevity of these gardens has already exceeded most technologies, even though they seldom pay their way and would soon die without our interest, participation, and love.

Study the motivations that were behind the creation of these fine gardens and you may see God's Ideas coming through His

Servants of Change. He gave us two brains to use, the logical left brain and the right brain for our creative use, for ideas.

"The only two things really important in life are Ideas and the Perseverance to follow them through," said the Contemporary Artist of Change, Count Bernadotte, who created the garden isle of Mainau. This magnificent garden and ecological site will probably last a thousand years. Listen and watch him, he is still alive, writing and creating.

GARDEN	LONGEVITY
Alhambra	760 years
Hampton Court	460 years
Hellbrunn	380 years
Cawdor Castle	370 years
Vaux-le-Vicomte	350 years
Herrenhausen	275 years
Bagatelle	220 years
Salzburg	200 years
Powerscourt	150 years
Mainau	140 years
Roseraie	110 years

Vaux-le-Vicomte, though planned by an over-ambitious man, greedy for power, was designed by a creative genius, André Le Nôtre. This garden, the author of this book believes, is the finest product of this landscape architect's creative mind, surpassing all that he planned later on.

M. Gravereaux's idea of making a beautiful rose garden to depict the history of the rose at the Roseraie in Paris was the result of this businessman's creative genius. A rose garden, as such, was a new idea at that time. This framework, a gorgeous garden, showing how roses from many parts of the world came to Europe, was a truly creative inspiration.

The owner of the great estate of Powerscourt, Ireland, traveled all over Italy and Germany looking for ideas, as well as actual artifacts, to bring back for the inspiration of his great Italianate terraces.

Truth is another flower on God's tree that produces change. Watch a small truth in this book cause a room in Spain to disappear.

Read behind the scenes in the author's ninety year love of gardens unfold here. You'll soon realize that her research and writing allows a better look at the Creator's Hand at Work in His World.

R. H. (Dick) Myers

Acknowledgments

I am very grateful to my dear late husband, James L. McFadden, who joined me so enthusiastically in vis– iting and photographing gardens during his business trips in Europe. We turned some of our pictures into a slide program called *Personalities Behind Some Fine Gardens of Europe*, and discovered it was our most popular show because it was about *people.*

When I showed it to my friend, Dick Myers, who lives in a world of new ideas, he suggested it would make a fascinating book, so I put the twelve most interesting stories together for *Drama in the Garden*. He has been most helpful in making suggestions for improvements page by page while I was working on it.

God must have approved of what I was doing, for from the very beginning, strange "coincidences" kept dropping more valuable material about the gardens in my lap.

The title was suggested by my dear late friend, Pat

Ziehbarth. I hope she is watching its progress from heaven!

I am also grateful for all the help my friend Carol Primmer gave me, finding the right library books for my research.

Many friends gave me encouragement, especially Lois Curley and Pearl Silvernale who critiqued every chapter for me. Other friends in various countries helped.

Our dear Parisian friends, Rene and Suzanne Lauret, drove us to see Vaux-le-Vicomte when it was not even mentioned in French guidebooks. They solved one problem after another for me as I wrote the three chapters on French gardens. Finally even their daughter, Elisabeth Bougault, spent much time to pin down some vital facts for me.

My English friend, Doreen Desty, and her professor/husband tracked down just the data I needed for the history of King Henry VIII's carved stone "beasties" at Hampton Court from the "Historic Palaces" archives and the Heraldry Society.

In my three years of efforts at finding Daniel Robertson's achievements before he was called to Powerscourt, I am especially grateful to Mary O'Farrell of the Irish Tourist Board in Dublin and Ann Simmons, Secretary of the Irish Architectural Archive in Dublin, who sent me extensive written material about the man's record as an architect.

The present owner of Levens Hall, Hal Bagot has been most helpful. The genealogical writings of his mother, Annette Bagot, F.S.A., were invaluable in writing this chapter.

When I needed more data about Cawdor Castle, my friend Sir Ilay Campbell sent me his delightful writings of Cawdor's history, as his Campbell clan had its seat there for many years. The well-known Scottish garden writer, Dawn MacLeod, was most helpful with her writings and suggestions.

For the story of Herrenhausen, I owe much to my cousin Gerd Eigenwillig's finding the excellent biography of Sophie. (Fortunately I read German easily.)

I am grateful for the happy hours my friend Didi Hegenauer and I spent together, photographing the Mirabell gardens in Salzburg, and for memories of much laughter as our grandchildren Bill and Charon (aged 10 and 8) dodged the "water jokes" at Hellbrunn.

As for the Alhambra, I am indebted to my friend Marylou Donnell. At least half of that chapter was written by her.

My daughter, Jean McFadden Willenberg, has been a constant joy for her enthusiasm about the book, and her willingness to contribute the line drawings and maps that I needed, as well as the Little Owl logo.

Since this is my first venture in self-publishing, I cannot express my gratitude enough to my production manager, Rex Heftmann, without whose expertise in computer layout and graphics, and business sense, I could not have produced this book. My thanks also to Dan Poynter whose excellent book, *The Self-Publishing Manual*, has been a wonderful guide.

God bless all these helpful people!

Dorothy Loa McFadden
Summer, 1992

Country Maps of these Twelve Gardens of Europe

You'll find small maps at the edge of the pages to help plan (or revise) your itinerary.

The attractions, eateries, and transportation may have changed, and many of the gardens host special events or seasonal programs which may affect your travel plans.

When you plan your tour and then again, the day before you visit, it's always a good idea to call ahead to confirm the hours and conditions at the gardens.

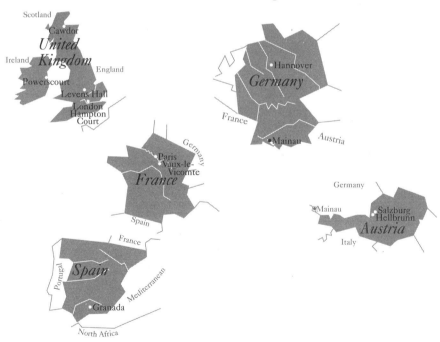

The Gardens

NICHOLAS FOUQUET

THE GARDEN IN COLOR ON PAGE 98

Chapter 1

Vaux-le-Vicomte
Melun, France

The Garden Party that Put the Host in Jail (for the Rest of his Life)

A s a host and planner of elaborate garden fêtes throughout history, surely none surpassed France's Nicolas Fouquet at his new establishment, Vaux-le-Vicomte (pronounced *vo-le-vee-cont´*), not far from Paris. Fouquet was Minister of Finance to King Louis XIV, and a prominent man of fashion, a lover of women, money and power. When Cardinal Mazarin died, Fouquet intensified his intrigues aimed at becoming his successor as First Minister, powerful ruler of France. But he failed in that ambition, as the King simply abolished Mazarin's post. Neither Fouquet nor the others surrounding the youthful king realized Louis' steely determination to be in full control himself.

The device on Nicolas Fouquet's crest was that of a squirrel, and like that lively creature, he was intent on climbing to the top. As his first leap, he decided to impress the King with his wealth and splendid surroundings, so in 1656 he began building an imposing chateau with extensive gardens at Maincy, near Melun.

Fouquet was a man of many talents and a good understanding of law and diplomacy. As an active patron of the arts, he surrounded himself with some of the finest creative minds living in Paris. He was the leader of intellectual society. So for his new venture, he enlisted the help of three of his friends: architect Louis Le Vau, decorator Charles Le Brun, and landscape architect André Le Nôtre, later to become known as "The Gardener of Kings and King of Gardeners."

Neither Fouquet nor his trio of designers considered cost in dreaming up this extraordinary architectural and horticultural creation. Fouquet's position as financial head of France gave him access to great sums of money. Never had so much talent and creative genius been combined in France to produce such a chateau and vast pleasure grounds for a man of wealth. Fouquet employed some 2000 men for the work, and had three villages and two small streams relocated to make way for the channeling of water to his many fountains and pools.

After five years of construction, in 1661, the work was finished. He had shown it to the King. But his majesty was quite sure that the funds to create this chateau and garden had been taken from the French treasury, and he talked the matter over with Colbert. They had already decided to arrest Fouquet and try him in court. So now they suggested to Fouquet that he arrange a great fête at Vaux-le-Vicomte for the entire court, and that the King would be delighted to return then to see any new embellishments that had been added. So some 2000 came, making an enormous crowd with their servants and horses. The fête began in the afternoon, with the gaily dressed company strolling about in the great gardens.

They stopped first on the viewing terrace at the front

DRAMA IN THE GARDEN

of the chateau, to gaze in amazement at the vastness and beauty of the garden design. Never had they seen anything like it. This was the first of André Le Nôtre's great gardens, the initial outburst of his original genius, which has never been surpassed, in the opinion of some experts, or if so, only by his later creations at Versailles.

Vaux-le-Vicomte was not the first of the formal, geometrical gardens of France, there had been some at Richelieu, Rueil, St. Cloud and St. Germain. But the vision which Le Nôtre had for Vaux-le-Vicomte was extraordinary. The vast concept was conceived on paper with ruler and triangle, planned for its quiet dignity, its balanced proportions, its discipline and order. Le Nôtre was a creator with a very precise, linear vision. It was during this period that the gardens created for large estates were all planned to be of great size as they were used like outdoor ballrooms for enormous parties.

The guests standing in front of the chateau could overlook the entire plan, yet as they descended the stairs and moved along on the great wide avenues, or took paths to one side or the other, going up or down a few occasional steps, they were constantly surprised by new features, garden pools, statues, or grottoes which they had not noticed before. It was as if they were turning the pages of a huge picture book, with new beauty always ahead. Variety delighted them between the rigidly outlined lawns and the more graceful parterre patterns. At that time nobody had ever seen such a display of statuary in a French garden. The climax, the dramatic focal point of the whole scene, was the great pool at the lower end, and then still higher on a gentle slope, the enormous statue of Hercules glittering in the afternoon light. (The original sculpture by Puget was lost. A later owner, M. Sommier, had it replaced by the one created by Farnesi, which we see today.)

As the sunset colors began to fade, the guests drifted into the chateau for the banquet. This was served on silver-gilt plate. Later on, a new play written in three weeks' time for the fête by Molière was presented in the garden, "Les Facheux", with the author playing the leading role.

The grounds were skillfully illuminated with torches for the throngs of admiring guests as they strolled and chatted, flirted and enjoyed the fabulous affair. Some writers describing the fête wrote that the high point of the night arrived when an enormous "whale" suddenly rose out of the great pool at the far end of the garden, spouting flames and smoke. At the same moment the sky filled with an extraordinary display of fireworks, man-made stars and comets whizzing up and curving back to earth from various corners of the garden, accompanied by a resounding cannonade which reminded some of the guests of the thunders of battle.

King Louis was indeed impressed, but not pleased by what he had seen. By the time gifts of diamond tiaras and splendid saddle horses were presented to many favored guests, Louis was so filled with a mixture of envy and anger that he could hardly contain himself. He refused his host's invitation to sleep in the royal suite which had been prepared for him, and drove hastily back to Fontainebleau with his mother, Queen Ann of Austria, arriving there at dawn.

Not long after, he had Fouquet seized and thrown into prison. Fouquet's friends stood by him and managed to print great quantities of papers elsewhere in Fouquet's defense, and circulate them around Paris. A special court was set up to try him, at which papers (probably forged) were shown, accusing Fouquet of plotting to overthrow the throne.

His trial dragged on for three years, as Fouquet tried

DRAMA IN THE GARDEN

courageously to defend himself. Public opinion favored him to a great extent. La Fontaine, the famous author of  fables, even wrote an ode urging leniency towards him. Finally Fouquet was sentenced to banishment, or freedom outside of France , with 9 votes for death and 13 for banishment) but the King broke the judge's decision and had him jailed for life. There Fouquet languished miserably until his death nineteen years later. The squirrel

WANDERING IN VAUX-LE-VICOMTE
Photo by Dorothy Loa McFadden, APSA

had made his last leap and had fallen, never to rise again.

Fouquet's widow stayed at Vaux until 1705, when the estate was sold, and then passed through several hands. Finally the chateau was to be auctioned off and torn down, but when the time came, a sugar magnate named Alfred Sommier bought it, and started the estate's renovation. It was almost entirely restored to its former elegance by the time M. Sommier died in 1908. The chateau itself is today a beautiful treasure, open to the public, filled with exquisite furniture, paintings, art objects, many originals from the genius of LeBrun. Sommier's descendants continued to put the garden back into its original plan. We owe a great debt of gratitude to this family for their generosity and wisdom in bringing this unique estate back to its original beauty. They now reside in part of the chateau. They have organized an association, "Les Amis de Vaux-le-Vicomte," which contributes to the upkeep of the estate and encourages visitors and research projects in the arts.

For the architect and designer of Fouquet's chateau, and especially for the genius who had planned the garden, André Le Nôtre, this extravagant party of Fouquet's marked the beginning of a new life. The King took them all under his wing and soon had them working on his palace and grounds at Versailles, which he was determined to make the largest and most imposing in Europe. From Vaux-le-Vicomte itself he appropriated for his own use great wagon loads of tapestries, brocade curtains, silver ornaments, many of the statues from the garden, and over 1000 of the lemon and orange trees. (The King was inordinately fond of lemon trees and had them placed in silver tubs in every room of his palaces.) In spite of this draining away of many of its treasures, the garden at Vaux-le-Vicomte today is still one of the finest and most beautiful in Europe. Nicolas Fouquet's dreams of political power were never realized, but by his brilliant choice of really creative artist designers, he left his mark on the gardens of Europe for many long years.

DRAMA IN THE GARDEN

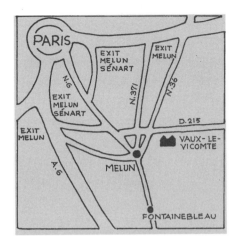

VAUX-LE-VICOMTE

JMW

Tips for Travelers

Location: 35 miles south-east of Paris; 12 miles from Fontainebleau; 3 miles from Melun.

Transportaion: By major tour buses from Paris; or driving from Paris on route A-4 or A-6, exit Melun-Senart-Melun;at Melun exit N.36.

Open: April 1-Nov.1 daily from 10 A.M.to 5 ; November to March weekend afternoons 2 P.M.-5 P.M. Closed December & January.

Admission Fee: Admission to castle, gardens & carriage museum, 42 F.F., or for gardens only, 20 F.F.

No guided tours except for groups making arrangement in advance with guide suggested by the estate tourist office.

Gift Shop: with postcards, slides, books etc.

Events: Saturdays of each month from 3-6 P.M. Candlelight Evenings every Saturday from June to September,when the Chateau is open from 8:30-11 PM to view over 1000 lighted candles. On these evenings the fine cafeteria and the Carriage Museum are also open. The Carriage Museum exhibits fine examples made by the coach builders of the 18th and 19th centuries.

Refreshments: The sunny terrace and the quaint "Squirrel" cafeteria (complete with a "micro-ondes"–microwave oven!) in the out-buildings are inviting for meals or snacks.

The Garden Party that Put the Host in Jail

GARDEN STATUARY
Photo by Dorothy Loa McFadden, APSA

THE GARDEN IN COLOR ON PAGE 99

Chapter 2
Bagatelle
Paris, France

MARIE-ANTOINETTE

When Marie-Antoinette
Lost a Bet

According to one French writer, the frivolous crowd gathered around Louis XVI and Marie-Antoinette at the French court looked like "so many pet monkeys capering about and seeking pleasures that inescapably ended with boredom." This was the atmosphere in which the still beautiful chateau and gardens of Bagatelle were built.

The story is an amusing one, typical of the high-flown extravagance of the court and its entourage that was ultimately to lead to the guillotine, for Marie-Antoinette was to end not merely losing her wager but also her pretty head.

It happened in 1777. The Count d'Artois, Louis XVI's youngest brother, and, rumor had it, wildly in love with his sister-in-law, was at the tender age of 18 already married with numerous mistresses besides. One day, when chatting gaily with Marie-Antoinette, she began to tease

27

him about having bought the land of Bagatelle with its old, dilapidated chateau. The Count was suddenly overcome by a mad impulse and offered the Queen a wager.

"Let me build you a little chateau there, a trifle, a bagatelle if you will, surrounded by beautiful gardens to make a fitting frame for your delicate beauty. It could serve as an enchanting setting for your receptions as well as a discreet hideaway for a rendez-vous for two. I'll wager you 100,000 pounds it'll be completed within 2 months while you're at Versailles. I invite you to a party there in exactly 60 days from now. If not, I will pay you 100,000 pounds. Will you take me on?"

Marie-Antoinette burst out laughing. But she accepted the wager, sure that not the smallest chateau, even without the gardens, could be completed in two months. Secretly, she was thinking of all the jewels she could buy with those 100,000 pounds. Was it to be that magnificent necklace, set with precious gems, that she had noticed a short while back in a jeweler's shop? Or perhaps some gorgeous dresses in which to dazzle her many admirers?

And so she set out for Versailles in the company of the King and his courtiers, weighing the respective values of these two things that she longed for. Meanwhile the Comte d'Artois wasted no time. He purchased a large property in the Bois de Boulogne, set among other properties with their own follies. He hired the services of a celebrated architect, Belanger, and ordered him to build an exquisite house in white stone. He asked a sculptor to create two sphinxes to guard the main entrance staircase, the sphinxes to be modeled after some he had seen at the home of one of his mistresses..

Thomas Blaikie, his Scottish landscape architect, was commissioned to design and decorate a great park of 6,000 square meters in the new English "landscape style." What was called a "garden" in England at that time was a new concept, consisting of great sweeps of lawns, tiny hills topped with little temples or sculpture, no flowers at all. The idea was sweeping all of Europe. (The result was what we in America would not call a "garden" at all. These to our minds are "parks.") It was a new concept for the French as well, who were still under the spell of Le Nôtre's geometrical order and formality in garden design.

Work began immediately, the old residence was demolished, land was cleared and the building of the chateau began. But all this was too slow for the Comte d'Artois. He took things into his own hands. He inspected, criticized, added new touches. Soon his project began to take shape at a smart pace. Some 900 workmen toiled day and night. They enjoyed a constant supply of wine to keep their spirits up. Bagpipes and barrel organs poured out an endless stream of gay music, rain or shine, in the sun or by torchlight. So much material was required that the Count was forced to use extreme measures. His Swiss guards confiscated all the wagon loads of lime, stone and good soil that passed through the streets, to use for the building of Bagatelle. Although the Comte did pay for these, there was much protest among the citizens of Paris.

BAGATELLE, ROSE GARDEN
Photo by Dorothy Loa McFadden, APSA

Amazing as it may seem, the work was finished on time. It had cost the Count some 700,000 pounds, but he had won the wager. When Marie-Antoinette and her friends arrived for the promised party, and wandered about the lovely landscape, they were delighted. The Queen gaily paid her admirer the 100,000 pounds he had won, for here was a new, delightful setting which she and her court could enjoy.

The Count d'Artois, unlike his beloved Marie-Antoinette, escaped the guillotine, as he was living for

NEW AND OLD
Photo by Dorothy Loa McFadden, APSA

some time in Great Britain.. After he returned, he became King of France as Charles X in 1824, but abdicated in favor of his son, and was exiled to Prague where it was said he repented of his misspent youth., and turned to religion. He had all the erotic paintings in the chateau of Bagatelle painted over.

During Napoleon's reign the chateau became his hunting lodge. The property then passed through the ownership of various British aristocrats. In 1905, Bagatelle was purchased by the City of Paris.

Thus began a new era for Bagatelle., mainly through the influence of one man, Jean-Claude Nicolas Forestier, whose effigy is engraved on a medallion in the Iris Garden. After holding various positions in the Paris Department of Parks and Gardens, he was appointed Curator of the Bois de Boulogne, and was responsible for nature conservancy for Bagatelle. He was a friend of artist Claude Monet and a great admirer of his Impressionist paintings and his lovely garden in Givenchy, so he introduced a waterlily pool and a profusion of flowers to the grounds of Bagatelle, planting great blocks of color and creating subtle harmonies or strong contrasts. In 1906 he created Bagatelle's famous Rose Garden, asking all the rose growers of France to contribute specimens. One of these was M. Jules Gravereaux, creator of the unique garden of the history of the rose, *L'Hay-les-Roses*, (See Chapter 3 in this book.) M. Gravereaux donated to the city of Paris several hundred species and different varieties of roses. Forestier arranged the final 9000 roses of 1000 varieties in a beautiful formal French garden. It includes polyanthus, floribundas, hybrid teas, climbers, bushes, and weeping rose trees. New prize winners are added annually when the Bagatelle International New Rose Competition is held.

Bagatelle is still one of Paris' favorite places for a stroll, a relaxed time among the flowers. In the spring there are thousands of bulbs in bloom; June is the high spot for the Rose Garden and the Iris Garden; summer is the time for the waterlilies and magnolias and many annuals; and in the fall there are dahlias, geraniums and asters, as well as many fine trees in their colored autumn foliage. Even in winter there is color, with many berries on pyracantha, hollies, and the first showing of snowdrops and crocus.

The chateau is not open to the public.

Tips for Travelers

Getting there: You may take the metro (subway) #1 line, to station Porte Maillot; or the Autobus #244 marked "to Porte Maillot," and get off at "Pre Catalan."

Admission Fee: O.50 F

Refreshments: There is a restaurant.

M. JULES GRAVEREAUX

THE GARDEN IN COLOR ON PAGE 100

Chapter 3
Roseraie
Paris, France

A *Living History* *of the Rose*

Who would have thought that a French businessman who became a millionaire would produce two radically new ideas in the world of horticulture? He not only created the first rose garden of the time in Europe, but he had it designed to illustrate the history of the rose.

It was M. Jules Gravereaux, retired co-owner of the popular and successful Parisienne department store, Bon Marche, which is still thriving today.

In 1888, he brought forth these two unique, absolutely new ideas. At that time, roses were grown here and there in gardens for the purpose of cutting and presenting them as a hostess gift or anniversary present. M. Gravereaux was fond of roses, so he bought some land and planted a few, supplementing them with gifts he solicited from friends near and far. In 1898 the collection became so large that he enlisted the help of the famous landscape designer, Edouard Andre, to create a decorative garden. This became a carefully planned history of the rose called L'Hay-les-Roses (pronounced *laileroz*.) By 1900 there were three thousand varieties. The many uses of the rose, popular today, were completely new at that time: roses in baskets, grafted on high stems, trained as tree roses, on trellises, pillars, etc.

In 1901 M. Gravereaux traveled to the roses' countries of origins and made trips for the Ministry of Agriculture to Serbia, Bulgaria, Asia Minor, and Turkey, bringing back samples of plants and important documents which taught the process of extraction of rose essence for perfumes. Visitors can now see many roses of the Far East in one part of the garden and the heavily scented roses in a special collection of roses Gallico. Another section of the garden displays the roses that were cultivated by the Empress Josephine at Malmaison. Still other plantings display the best foreign roses developed by horticulturists of the world in the 19th and 20th centuries.

In 1905, when the city of Paris decided to add a rose garden to Bagatelle (see Chapter 2) the landscape designer in charge, J.C.N. Forestier, asked for assistance from M. Gravereaux, who immediately donated a large number of roses.

In 1906 he created a Theatre of the Rose in the garden, presenting there the first of his annual Fetes de Rosali, featuring ballet dancers from the Opera and the Opera Comique.

In that same year, the community of l'Hay, proud of this beautiful garden, changed its name to l'Hay des Roses.

M. Gravereaux also established a delightful little museum in the garden, filled with every book about the rose, paintings and ornaments of all kinds which featured the rose. Unfortunately this was vandalized and later burned down when the house was destroyed by fire. He published many horticultural pamphlets and books about his favorite flower.

Jules Gravereaux died in his home on March 23, 1916, mourned by his family, grandchildren, and many friends, especially the members of the French Rose Society. He was remembered as a true, honest gentleman, generous and kind.

According to R.C.Balfour, M.B.E., D.H.M., past president of the R.N.R.S in England and of the World Federation of Rose Societies, "the Roseraie is certainly one of the finest and most important rose gardens of the world."

The garden property was bought in 1968 by the city's department of Val-de-Marne, which added a section for showing the best of the new roses each year. The garden is a popular park for residents of Paris who also enjoy the splendid old trees throughout the property. During the end of May and through June as one walks among the overarching bloom amid the showers of color and breathing in the overwhelming fragrance, one indeed feels he is in a little paradise where reigns the queen of flowers, the rose.

Tips for Travelers

Address: Rue Albert-Watel. 94240, L'Hay des Roses, Paris

Transportation: Take Bus 172 ,or metro Villejuif and get off at station Aragon. Or Bus 172 and 192, get off at station RER Bourg-la-Reine.

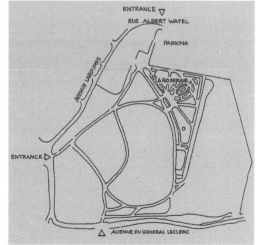

ROSERAIE

Open: May 11 to September 23 daily from 10 A.M. to 6 P.M. Best flowering: end of May through June.

Admission fee: 6 F

Telephone: 47.40.04.04.

JMW

THE KING'S DRAGON
Photo by Dorothy Loa McFadden

THE GARDEN IN COLOR ON PAGE 101

Chapter 4
Hampton Court
England

King Henry VIII and His Beasties

Today, visitors to the vast, beautiful gardens of Hampton Court near London could not possibly envision what it looked like in 1529 when King Henry VIII took it over from his chief advisor, Cardinal Wolsey. He wanted to impress his personality immediately on everything in the palace itself and in the grounds so he ordered a new garden to be created according to his ideas. We are grateful for the research of the late Nan Fairbrother for her delightful book, *Men & Gardens*, in which she wrote, "There were flower gardens overflowing with primroses, violets, gilly-flowers, and Sweet Williams costing three pence for a hundred, roses at four pence each." These were watered each night by gardeners who dipped buckets full from the nearby River Thames.

But his favorite garden, which he proudly showed off to every visitor no matter what time of day or night they

37

arrived, was his garden of the "mount." These "mounts" were very popular in Tudor times, consisting of little artificial hills which, to quote Nan Fairbrother "climbed by a path edged with hawthorn bushes which circled the slope like 'turnings of cokil-shells.' On the top there was a summer-house, and judging by the bills for glazing the windows, it must have been quite large enough for a family to live in." But Henry's chief delight was not in flowers, but in his 'beasties'–fantastic carved figures of animals painted and gilt stone, which sat on the tops of posts set everywhere about the gardens. Often they held banners and it must have been very cheerful and very ridiculous.

Certainly the mound garden which the King adored would seem very cluttered and confusing to us today with its riot of colors. The poles holding the stone beasts were striped like barber poles in green and white, since green was the royal color. The garden was surrounded by picket fences also painted alternately green and white.

There were twenty brass sundials, columns and pyramids of wood, trellises, and so on and on. But to Henry and the people surrounding him, the stone beasties were a very serious matter for they portrayed the coats of arms of royalty.

There was the King's Lion, the Queen's Unicorn, the King's Greyhound, the Queen's Lion, the King's Bull, the Queen's Yale, the King's

Dragon, the Queen's Panther. They lined the path to the Mound garden, as well as being set into the garden itself in great profusion. Some of the decorations on the beasts' pennants had to be changed as Henry's wives were executed, died, or were divorced and a new queens' emblems must be portrayed. For economy's sake, the records show, when Queen Anne's beast was altered for Queen Jane, it was done by "new makyng of hedds and the taylls." Many of the original beasts have vanished. Today the survivors are on each side of the parapets as one goes toward the entrance of the palace, which was created and installed in 1909 when the moat was cleared and the bridge restored.

These are, on the left parapet:

1. The crowned lion of England, with the impaled arms of Henry VIII and Queen Jane.

2. A panther, with the Seymour wings.

3. A greyhound with collar and leash, bearing the three lions of England.,

4. A yale, with Queen Jane's coat of augmentation.

5. A dragon, with an uncrowned portcullis.

On the right-hand parapet:

6. A unicorn, with Queen Jane's six-quartered shield.

7. A dragon, with the royal arms, New France and England quarterly.

8. A lion wearing a coronet of formy crosses and fleur de lis and holding a shield with Queen Jane's badge.

9. A bull, with a Tudor rose.

10. A panther, with the impaled arms as held by the lion of England.

These beasts unfortunately weathered badly, and had to be replaced in 1950.

(We are indebted to the Archives of the Royal Palaces for the above notes.)

In his youth Henry was slender, handsome and athletic, and he had a fine tennis court built where he could play before an admiring audience. This is still among the popular sights at Hampton Court today. Tennis, at that time, was played with a hard ball, off the walls. He also had a tiltyard of nine acres built for jousting, where he made spectacular leaps from horse to horse, winning much applause from his audience in the observation towers. The Tiltyard Gardens are of particular interest to horticulturists, with double-sided herbaceous borders and experimental planting.

THE GREAT
VINE

Another attraction is the Maze, planted in Henry's day, which is still enjoyed by visitors young and old. The author's grandson Billy, at age ten, skipped through it happily in a very short time. But many adults get lost and do not find their way out for quite a while.

Another thing to see today is the ancient Black Hamburgh grape vine, now over 100 years old, which was planted by Capability Brown. The girth of the vine at ground level now measures more than seven feet with some branches 114 feet long. Tradition has it that its roots go all the way into the Thames. It still produces over 600 pounds of fine grapes each year which are sold to the public. The fascinating little Knot Garden, which was first created here for Henry, is designed in the old tradition to be enjoyed from a window looking down.

Certainly Hampton Court's beautiful, extensive gardens, 67 acres, are worth a whole day of any tourist's itinerary. There are so many fine flower borders, interesting trees, ponds and pools, tempting walks, and bird varieties that are a delight for any garden lover. Whether you simply enjoy the King's beasties or want to study their heraldic meanings, they will look down at you benignly and tell you to make the most of these fine gardens created so long ago.

Tips for Travelers

Going to Hampton Court: By river barge from the center of London, Westminster Pier, 90 minutes. By public transport trains from Waterloo BR, 35 minutes. Frequent bus services.

Admission fee: To palace & gardens, adults $8.00, children $5.00. Admission to Maze, adults $2.15, children $1.45

Information: Telephone: 081- 977- 8441

Lodgings: If you wish to sleep in this royal palace, inquire of Britain's Landmark Trust about the two apartments being made available for rent (notice in *U.S. News and World Report* magazine November 2, 1992). No phone or TV, bathroom facilities complicated!

Restaurant: The Tiltyard, lunches under $25.00, English Teas under $10.00

Gift Shop: Offers many books.

THE PRESENT OWNERS OF LEVENS HALL, HAL AND SUSAN
BAGOT WITH JESSICA, LAURA, RICHARD, AND HARRY.
Photo by Lucy Sclater

THE GARDEN IN COLOR ON PAGE 102

Chapter 5

Levens Hall
Lake District, England

JMW

Laughter in the Garden

Nobody touring the Lake District of England should miss visiting Levens Hall. This beautiful mansion and garden is unique in Great Britain. Where else can you visit a "stately home" filled with priceless historical objects, decorated walls and ceilings, beside a garden of humorous topiary planted in 1694! And hear about ghosts appearing even today—yet still feel that you are being warmly welcomed to a friendly family home?

The family, now living there, take the appearance of their ghosts very lightly. One of Hal Bagot's sisters, Lisa Bagot, saw the "Grey Lady" when she was seven years old, describing her costume accurately, though never having seen a gypsy. Many guests and members of the family have been startled by a black woolly dog which runs in front of their legs and disappears in the guest room above. Perhaps most interesting of all is the fact that the previous owner, Mr. Robin Bagot, was once heard playing his harpsichord in Levens Hall when he was actually in Keswick! These stories are told in the visitors' guidebook "in order to amuse, alarm or entertain."

But let us enter the Great Hall, and browse among its treasures: the 16th century plaster work and panelling, armor from the Civil Wars, an Arabian saddle belonging to Elphi Bey, in whose palace Napoleon lived during the Egyptian campaign. Over the fireplace is the coat-of-arms of Elizabeth I, and around the frieze are those of the Bellingham family from 1307-1688. There is a lovely Florentine painting by Bicci di Lorenzo of the Madonna and Child, dated about 1430 by Berenson. A beautifully written and illustrated booklet gives the visitor details about all these priceless items, leading on through the many rooms.

It is fortunate that the present owners inherited a wealth of papers about Levens Hall from the time of Colonel Grahme, which are still being studied by the family as well as by students poring over them at the County Record Office.

It was Colonel Grahme who added various improvements to the buildings at Levens Hall, but his great contribution was employing Monsieur Guillaume Beaumont to design and supervise the planting of the grounds.

Beaumont was a pupil of Le Nôtre (See Chapter 1 in this book) and had been employed by King James II to design Hampton Court (see Chapter 4 in this book) and planned the estates of many prominent landowners. He came to Levens Hall in 1689, at the time when James II abdicated, and Col. Grahme had also lost his position as keeper of the Privy Purse and Keeper of the buckhounds for the king. Together these two men spent many enthusiastic years creating the gaiety and beauty of Levens Hall's grounds which even then drew visitors from miles around, in spite of the dreadful muddy roads.

When one looks at the portraits painted of these two men, one might think they were both of very somber dispositions. But Col. Grahme apparently was full of a

TOPIARY FORMS
Photo by Dorothy Loa McFadden, APSA

bubbling sense of humor, showing in the whimsical topiaries which we still see in the garden today, some twelve feet tall: there are cones and corkscrews, circles and pyramids, a huge umbrella and hat, a group called "Queen Elizabeth and her maids," a lion, and a huge one known as "The Judge's Wig." It used to take four men three months to clip the topiary, and even now with electric clippers, it takes four men six weeks.

Fortunately Col. Grahme's daughter, Catherine Countess of Suffolk and Berkshire, doggedly insisted during her old age that nothing designed by Beaumont should be changed. But succeeding owners allowed the grounds to go literally to seed, and finally a later gardener had to replant nine miles of box edging which had gotten out of hand. However, the main problem for the preservation of Beaumont's great design came in modern times, when the present owner's father was forced to devote six years to preventing the end of the park from being destroyed by a proposed link road through the focal point. He finally won, and the Ministry in 1970 announced the route of the present Kendal link to the motorway M6, leaving this unique example of a late-seventeenth century landscape design intact.

The beautiful garden which we see today is colorful with polyanthi and pansies below the topiary in spring, followed by summer bedding plants, and roses in an enchanting section with a ginkgo tree towering over them, and a recent metrasequoia, flanked by wisteria and other colorful climbers. The forebears of the present owner planted a long border beyond the topiary garden, with climbers and old fruit trees hugging the wall, and flowering shrubs and a grey border. Opposite and beyond the topiary there is a small Secret Garden enclosed by yew hedges. Other remnants of Beaumont's fine planning can still be seen in The Rondel, enclosed by beech hedges with four paths leading off on opposite sides. These beeches are enormous today, as impressive as the topiary, their light green leaves a lovely foil for the dark yews. There is also a mixed avenue aligned with one of the beech alleys, going off into the informally planted park, where the visitor can see one of the earliest examples in Britain of what is called a "ha-ha," a wide deep ditch which prevents the farm animals from crossing to the gardens.

There is another delightful story about Col. Grahme, full of "laughter in the garden." He was a very friendly, sociable person, keeping in close touch with the gentlemen owners in the neighborhood. They originated a tradition of entertaining each other at parties in their gardens and on a certain day in May each year, they all came to Levens Hall for a "Radish Feast." There would be a wheelbarrow full of freshly pulled radishes, brown bread, and plenty of the strong drink called "Morocco" brewed in the Levens Hall ale house of beer and herbs from a secret recipe. The mugs were probably often tossed about during the revelry, for one was found in recent years firmly imbedded in the high branches of a grotesque yew.

Levens Hall is an unusual stately home and garden, endowed with beauty within and without, and unusual friendly ghosts. We are happy that the owners keep it open for others to enjoy.

Tips for Travelers

Location: 5 miles south of Kendal off the A6, and north-west of the M6 (Junction 36.)

Open: Beginning Easter Sunday, Sundays to Thursdays 11 A.M. to 5 P.M. from Easter to end of September. Garden only is open weekdays in October.

Admission Fee: In 1992, -L-3.50 for adults, less for children and groups.

Special Exhibits: The Steam Collection, illustrating the development of industrial steam power from 1820-1920, in the former Brew House includes table engines, beam engines and hot-air engines, with a number of full-size engines. On Sundays & Bank Holidays a fine half-size Tractor Engine gives children rides around the grounds, on Sundays and Bank Holiday Mondays, and the full-size engines are in steam, weather permitting.

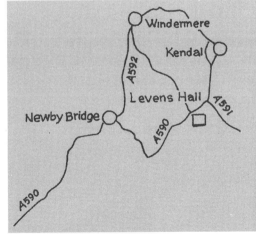

LEVENS HALL

Gift Shop: In the 13th century undercroft of the original Pele Tower.

Tea Room: Refreshments in the original panelled servants' hall. Home-made lunches and teas, wines, beer and ice-creams.

Play Area: for young children, within the topiary garden.

Laughter in the Garden

OXFORD PRESS, OXFORD, ENGLAND
Photo: Dorothy Loa McFadden, APSA

THE GARDEN IN COLOR ON PAGE 103

Chapter 6

Powerscourt
Enniskerry, Ireland

*The Gardener
in the
Wheelbarrow*

How many bottles of sherry were drained by the designer of these superb gardens at Powerscourt as he was pushed about in a wheelbarrow, supervising 100 workmen with their horsedrawn carts?

Daniel Robertson suffered from the gout, so he could not attempt to scramble about on the steep hillside. Each day he clutched a bottle of sherry to his chest, and when it was empty, work stopped for the day. The owner of this vast estate, the 6th Viscount Powerscourt, had engaged him in 1843 because of his reputation in both England and Ireland. Robertson was originally an architect, and had designed the fine classical building which still houses the Oxford Press. He was employed for both architectural work and garden design by a number of landowners in England. But he was addicted to alcohol and constantly in debt, so he had fled to Ireland, where he had planned architectural improvements and gardens for a number of prominent people.

The owner of the 36,000-acre estate, the Sixth Viscount Powerscourt, traveled around Europe absorbing ideas from splendid gardens, and bringing back exquisite wrought iron gates and railings and fine statuary for use in his garden in Ireland. He employed Daniel Robertson to design and supervise the splendid Italianate garden at Powerscourt.

There is an account of the development of the gardens, written by the Viscount at the time, which clearly shows how closely he worked with Daniel Robertson on every detail. He apparently had great faith in his talents and was tolerant of the little man's weaknesses and explosive temperament. So Robertson had himself taken around on the steep slope in a wheelbarrow, teetering precariously at times while hurling oaths at the man who was pushing him. As Lord Powerscourt recorded, there were often occasions when the sheriff's men came after Robertson trying to jail him for his debts, caused by his heavy drinking. But whenever word came of a sheriff approaching, the Viscount hid Robertson in the domes on the roof of his big mansion.

In the records, the Viscount's son remembered clearly how on his seventh birthday —a cold October morning in 1843— he was "dragged from his schoolroom to lay the first stone" of the great new garden terraces. This was at a terrible time in the history of Ireland, the time of the potato famine, when a million people died of five years of unemployment and starvation. Another million fled in desperation to other lands, mainly to America. So the Sixth Viscount, by giving work to over 100 men in the area, was doing great good as well as creating beauty on his land. When he died in 1844 on his way home from Italy, work on the garden stopped. It was not until fourteen years later, when the Seventh Viscount had come of age, that construction was resumed. Daniel Robertson had also died by then, so the Seventh Viscount employed another fine gardener, a Scot named Alexander Robertson, but not related to Daniel.

Like his father, the Seventh Viscount took an active part in the creation of the gardens. When he studied Daniel Robertson's plans for the four flights of granite steps leading down the central axis, he showed an unerring sense of scale. He realized that four consecutive steps of the same width would be too large, and monotonous. So he employed a well-known architect, Francis Penrose, to reduce their width and then to design the beautiful floor patterns of black and white pebbles — brought from the beach at Bray— which were imbedded in concrete in the Italian manner.

He solved another interesting problem with Alexander Robertson's help. Surface water came out of the slope and threatened to carry away the terraces. They found that in ancient times the land had been part of a glacier moraine and that (I quote from his account) "the ice, having carried down the gravel, had lain probably for centuries at certain levels, which were marked by thin coats of marl, impervious to water and which did not correspond with our terraces.

TRITON POOL
Photo by Dorothy Loa McFadden, APSA

Robertson suggested... that we should tap these marly deposits and dig holes through them, behind the terraces, so that the water inside, on coming out of these marly levels, should fall down through the holes into the next stratum and disappear. This was done, and we had no more trouble."

We who visit these beautiful gardens today certainly don't realize what complicated planning went into their creation, but we are grateful for the results. The handsome terraces lead down to the Triton Pool where two bronze winged horses commemorate the Wingfield family's coat of arms. (Sir Richard Wingfield had been granted this demesne in 1603 by King James I. He and his descendants were to hold it for 350 years.) The fountain throws its jet up 100 feet. Beyond one sees the beautiful backdrop of the mountains.

Wandering on one can enjoy the many magnificent trees planted years ago by successive owners and now extremely large. Many are unusual, such as the tallest Sitka Spruce in Great Britain, 174 feet high, and an Araucaria Cunningham —of the Monkey Puzzle family— which came from South America and is said to be the only one of its kind in Europe. There is a meadow perfect for a picnic, near the locale for many scenes in Sir Laurence Olivier's film of "Henry V."

In a grove beyond the woods a waterfall tumbles from a height of 398 feet, said to be higher than any other in Britain or Ireland.

Tips for Travelers

Location: 30 miles south of Dublin.

Transportation: Special tour buses from Dublin or a short drive by car.

Hours: Open: Daily 11A.M. to 6 P.M. from Easter to October. Sundays and Bank Holidays, 1:45 -6:15 P.M.

Admission Fee: Demesne and gardens, adults 2/6, children under 14, 6d. Waterfall: adults 1/-children 6d. Cars and motorcycles, 6d. per vehicle.

Tours: Half-hourly on Saturday afternoons, also Sundays, last tour on Bank Holidays and Sundays at 5:15 P.M. Groups of 20 or more, arranged in advance, 2/- per person. Pamphlet available to use for self-guiding.

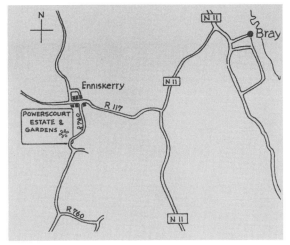

POWERSCOURT

Shops: Cut flowers and pot plants available in the gardens. Souvenir Shop near the entrance.

Restaurant: Stag's Head Cafe near entrance.

Attractions nearby: Don't miss seeing the very fine *Glasnevin Botanical Gardens* in Dublin. They are not only instructional, but laid out for beauty. The perennial borders are magnificent. The little rock garden is a gem- it could teach any home gardener how to lay out one at home, with its winding path and a surprise around every corner.

Then not very far away, there is a unique garden of *Mt. Usher* in Ashford, on the main Dublin-Rossare Road N11, 50 km from Dublin. Open daily from March 17-Oct.31, 10:30A.M.-6P.M. Phone: 0404-40116, or 0404-40205. Admission: Adults L2.20, children L1.70. Groups of 20 or more, L1.70 each. There is a spacious Tea Room overlooking the river and gardens, and a shopping courtyard. Mt. Usher is a perfect example of a garden which looks as if it had simply grown there naturally, yet its 20 acres include over 5000 different species of plants from all over the world, happily growing along the River Vartry.

County Wicklow is also famous for its *GARDEN FESTI-VALS.* In 1992 these will be held from June5–28, during which time some 50 great houses and their gardens will be open to the public. From July 16-19 there will also be an Arklow Garden of Ireland Festival. For details write to Tourist Information Office, Fitzwilliam Square, Wicklow Town, Co. Wicklow, Ireland.

CAWDOR CASTLE, FROM THE TOP OF THE TOWER,
Photo by Dorothy Loa McFadden, APSA

THE GARDEN IN COLOR ON PAGE 104

Chapter 7

Cawdor Castle
Scotland

CAWDOR

500 Year Old Legend Proven True Today

The legend about the building of Cawdor Castle goes back some 500 years to William, the third Thane of Cawdor, who had a strange dream while he was pondering where to locate his castle. In this dream he was told to load his gold and treasures on a donkey and let the beast wander at will. Wherever the donkey lay down under a tree to rest, that was where he should build his castle.

So William did this and the donkey lay down under a thorn tree. William built his castle on the spot, incorporating the tree within the tower. We can see the stump today. But the amazing end to this story is that the present owner, Lord Cawdor, had the stump carbon-dated and it actually is 500 years old!

There is another true tale about Cawdor Castle, involving a baby girl, Muriel, whose father had died before she was born and whose mother had died soon after

Muriel was born. So this baby had now become the heiress to the vast Cawdor lands. She was being cared for by her maternal grandmother at Kilverock. Learning of this, Archibald Campbell, the second Earl of Argyll and tenth chief of Clan Campbell, decided to kidnap her and marry her to his son, thus acquiring the Cawdor estate. He dispatched a band of Campbells to capture her. There was quite a fight in which it was said seven Campbell sons died. But fortunately the baby's nurse thought to brand the baby's hip with a red hot key and bit off the child's little finger, thus making it impossible for Archibald to substitute any baby he wished as the heiress. But this story has a good ending, for at the age of 12, Muriel was married to one of Archibald's sons. It was said that it was a happy union.

The lives of the Cawdors were constantly full of danger. Within 300 years, the third Thane's brother was killed in battle; the fourth Thane was murdered; the sixth Thane was ordered by the King to raze and destroy the castle of Lochindorb; the ninth Thane was offended when his brother-in-law Maclean of Duart Castle chained up the Thane's sister naked to a rock in the sea. He hunted him down and finally killed him with a knife. His sister-in-law was burned as a witch. And so the history of violence goes on until the brother-in-law of the thirteenth Thane (the brilliant translator of Rabelais) died of uncontrollable laughter on hearing of the restoration of King Charles II.

In 1622, Sir John Campbell, the thirteenth Thane and owner of the Cawdor estates, introduced great improvements in the management of its beautiful forests. These are some of the finest and most productive in the British Isles.

Sir John's successor, Sir Hugh, knighted in 1660 upon the restoration of King Charles II, was a poet with a pas-

sion for building. He made the enlargement and beauti-
fying of Cawdor Castle his life's work, transforming it
over a period of some 40 years from a defensive tower
into the harmonious, elegant and spacious mansion which
visitors enjoy seeing today. It is his coat of arms which
we see carved above the main entrance.

The oldest garden northeast of the castle was full of
soft fruits, flowers, and vegetables all mixed together.
The plants used for cooking were at first all of local
seed, but later such vegetables as French sorrel and
Turkish parsley were introduced. In 1850, Lady Cawdor
redesigned the rose-beds. By 1980 the kitchen garden
was producing too much for use in the castle, or even for
local markets, so it was greatly reduced. Elizabeth, wife
of the 24th Thane, undertook much replanting of the
gardens in the middle of the 20th century.

The present owner, Lord Cawdor, has made five nature Trails in these woods available to visitors, a pleasure
not usually found in visits to great mansions. Happily the
present Lord Cawdor and his wife are enthusiastic about
the gardens and have extended them greatly, adding
much beauty to the estate. They planted an interesting
maze where the old kitchen garden was. It was copied
from a mosaic floor in a Roman villa in Portugal and is set
with holly, surrounded by a laburnum walk, edged with
trimmed myrtles and yew. The ground is covered with
moss which the birds love to use for nesting material.

There is also a "knot garden" made of herbs and culi-
nary plants and an interesting "thistle garden" of over
twenty varieties. There is the Paradise Garden with a
fountain and only white flowers for an atmosphere of
true restfulness. Some fruit trees from earlier periods can
still be seen.

Clipped yew hedges are festooned in summer with the
pretty small flower called "Scottish Flame Flower,"

THE CASTLE FROM ABOVE
Tourism Department, Cawdor Castle

though it is really a native of Chile. In the 19th century the Cawdors stayed in the castle only for the hunting season in the fall so the gardens featured late-blooming herbaceous borders but eventually bulbs, flowering trees and shrubs were added for earlier bloom.

Visitors are always amazed at the fine gardens flourishing in what is, after all, a latitude north of Moscow. The reason is the fine fertile soil, a climate tempered by the Gulf Stream, a rainfall of 24 inches distributed throughout the year, and sunshine in summer for 18 hours a day. The present owners add the best reason of all: the excellent head gardener, Mr. Derek Hosie.

Walking away from the castle one can enjoy a steep wild garden between the castle and the rocky stream of the Cawdor Burn. This is a shaggy informal ramble of daffodils, primulas, azaleas, rhododendrons, and willows,

DRAMA IN THE GARDEN

CAWDOR CASTLE

set among tall old trees. The highest of these is a Wellingtonia, 160 feet tall.

Though the grounds of Cawdor Castle are exceptionally beautiful now, undoubtedly there will always be more delightful additions made by the present Lord and Lady Cawdor.

Tips for Travelers

Location: In Nairnshire, between Inverness and Nairn on route B 9090 off the A 96.

Open: Seven days a week from May 1–October 4. From 10 A.M.- 5:30 P.M. Phone: Cawdor 615. Fax: 06677 674

Admission Fee: to the castle, gardens and grounds: —L 3.50

Guide to castle interior: Buy "Room Notes," L 2.50, a delightful witty booklet written by Lord Cawdor. (They are also posted in each room.)

Recreation: Miniature golf and putting green. Five Nature Trails. Picnic in the park. Swings. Feed the ducks.

Refreshments: Ice cream from the snack bar. Meals and drinks at licensed restaurant.

Gift Shop: Fine selections, souvenirs of Cawdor and Scotland.

OLD ROSE GARDEN, MAINAU
Photo by Dorothy Loa MacFadden, APSA

THE GARDEN IN COLOR ON PAGE 105

Chapter 8

Island of Mainau
(pronounced "My-now⁗")
Germany

COUNTESS SONJA & COUNT LENNART
BERNADOTTE

A Great Gardener for Mankind

When█ Count Lennart Bernadotte of Sweden gave up his privileges as a prince to marry a commoner, he had no idea as to his future work or possibilities for making a living.

As we wander through the beautiful "garden island" of Mainau which is his creation, one can only marvel at his vision and his gradual development as a great "gardener for mankind."

He had a very difficult childhood. When one reads the account in his autobiography (in German), *Gute Nacht, Kleiner Prinz*, ("Good Night, Little Prince,") one can easily see why he rebelled against the rules and regulations imposed on Swedish royalty. He was imaginative and creative, an inheritance probably from his mother.

She was a former Russian princess (her marriage to his father was a strictly political affair) who resisted all the

A View of Land as seen from Mainau
Publicity Department, Mainau

formalities and rules under which she was supposed to live in Sweden. When Lennart was only five she gave up and divorced his father, shocking all the nobility in both Sweden and Russia.

Victoria, the German dowager queen, was Lennart's grandmother. She was married to the Swedish king. She took over responsibility for the boy, setting out the rules for every moment of his existence through a nanny who ruled over him in obedience to the grandmother's ideas throughout his childhood and adolescence. He lived in one dreary, cold castle after another, suffering intermittently from pneumonia. Even if he had not fallen in love with a commoner and lost his privileges by marrying her, he would never have fitted into the old-fashioned ways demanded of Swedish royalty.

After his marriage and rejection by the Swedish court, he was entirely without funds. He became a professional photographer and travelled a great deal to fulfill assignments. But when his great-grandmother died and deeded the island of Mainau to him and his father, a new life began.

His great-grandfather had planted a very fine arboretum on the island, which had drawn many visitors. There were exotic trees from all over the world, including the American sequoias, and the amazingly mild climate surrounding this island had even produced bananas on flourishing trees there. Then he realized that if he could add to this little island a fine garden, it could become a unique tourist attraction: a place for modern people to relax among the beauties of nature, to get away from the noise and stress of daily life.

But first he and his father faced an appalling task, as the vegetation on Mainau had become a real jungle. His great-grandmother had felt it her duty after her husband died to preserve everything as he had left it, so she prohibited anyone from cutting even a single branch. The fine exotic trees which her husband had collected from all over the world were soon choked by the remaining natural vegetation.

Count Bernadotte (having been restored to a royal title by his aunt, but still without funds) together with his father on his short visits, tackled the clearing almost single-handed. He studied agriculture and forestry. Gradually he introduced splendid beds of flowers and cleared beautiful views onto the lake.

His aim was to be a "gardener for mankind." He envisioned the island as a place of relaxation and refreshment for the public.

Through all these efforts, he became a world-renowned pioneer in the movement to preserve the natural environment of the earth. After the World War II, he convinced the German government to establish an organization to ensure the creation of green belts around every town and village, and encourage home owners to become enthusiastic gardeners. He headed that new organization for many years. He travelled all over the world speaking on environmental problems.

One of his triumphs was the restoration of the Bodensee (Lake Constance) in which the island of Mainau lies, from contaminated water to a clean, drinkable lake. This must have taken much effort by the Count to get cooperation from many people, as the lake is bordered by three countries: Germany, Austria, and Switzerland, but he achieved his fine goal.

Today Mainau has also become a vibrant cultural center, hosting monthly and annual gatherings which have produced the Mainau Charter, as well as the Mainau

THE CASTLE ON THE LAKE
Publicity Department, Mainau

Talks. The conclusion of these talks between Nobel prize winners and other intellectuals is held on Mainau. There are also meetings to reinforce the work of the international YMCA and many other civic organizations.

As we tourists wander about this "Flower Island," away from the noise and pressures of ordinary life, we are fulfilling what Count Bernadotte had dreamed of throughout the difficult years. We are surrounded by nature's beauty, breathing clean air, watching the children enjoying a garden planned especially for them. We are close to a paradise on earth.

Beginning in the early spring, when there are millions of tulip bulbs and spring flowers in bloom, the island is overflowing with color. In May one can also enjoy 200 varieties of rhododendrons in bloom. There are many favorite varieties in the old rose garden, with its charming staircase still intact. By late summer, we see 20,000 dahlias of 200 varieties in dramatic beds that are almost overwhelming. Visitors are encouraged to choose the Queen of Roses and the Queen of Dahlias. In the fall there is brilliant foliage in the arboretum.

Every month of the year there are exhibits and special programs to enjoy in different locations throughout the island, either outdoors or in various buildings or greenhouses: paintings or handicrafts, concerts, lectures on the cultivation of roses or on taking care of house plants, shows of holiday table decorations arranged by specialists, and unique programs connected with Advent and Christmas.

Visitors enjoy seeing the fine old Baroque castles and chapel, built between 1739 and 1746 by the Knights of the Teutonic Order. The island was their headquarters for more than five hundred years.

The Count is now concluding his autobiography while his wife, Countess Sonja, travels extensively to fill engagements for talks on ecology.

In 1974 he and his wife created a foundation which will continue to foster many of his ideas, based on his firm conviction that property demands responsibility. The foundation's purpose is to foster international public-spiritedness, especially in science, by establishing contacts between young and older scientists on an international level; to promote landscape conservation based on the 1961 "Green Charter of Mainau," activities of the German Horticultural Society and the German Council for Land Planning and Conservation; to promote scientific research in the field of geopolitics and ecology, national culture, and the national heritage.

The formation of this foundation embodies the guiding principles of this former "little prince:" "One must follow an idea with the greatest patience and perseverance." Truly this great man has given the world the fruits of his superb ideas.

Tips for Travelers

Getting to Mainau: By train, ship or bus. For information, contact DB-Bodensee Schiffsbetriebe, 7750 Konstanz, phone 07531/281389. (Family tickets, ship and train, etc.) Also Tourist Information Konstanz, 7750 Konstanz, phone 07531/284376 (two-way ticket & Mainau, bus ticket). Or Stadtwerke Konstanz, (Ferry and buses) 7750 Konstanz, phone 07531/8030.

Hotels and Camping: For information, contact Fremdenverkehrsverband (Tourist office) Bodensee-Oberschwaben, Schuetzenstrasse 8, 7750 Konstanz. Phone 07531/22232. (Note: The Lake Constance area is rich in wonderful places to visit!)

Address: Blumeninsel Mainau GmbH, D-7750 Insel Mainau, Phone 07531/303-0. Fax 07531/303-248.

Admission Fees: Spring & summer: Adults, *DM*10; Children 6-16, *DM*3; Students age 17 and up or military, *DM*6; Senior citizens 65 and up, *DM*10; Tourist in groups of 25 and up, *DM*10; Art exhibits,

MAINAU ON LAKE CONSTANCE
(CALLED *BODENSEE* IN GERMAN)

*DM*1. *Fall & winter:* Adults *DM*5; Children 6-16, Free. Exhibits, free. Season ticket (from 1 March '92 to 28 February '93) *DM*25. Family season ticket with children, for a year, from March 1 to the end of February of the next year, *DM*50.

Transportation: Train from mainland entrance to the parking lot, *DM*2.

Bicycles: Not allowed on island. May be parked at entrances.

Restaurants: Open year around. Reservations, phone 07531/303156. Closes Mondays at 6 P.M.

Guided Tours: April to September, meet at palace courtyard, 11:30 A.M. and 2:00 P.M. Tour lasts 1 hour. Adults, *DM*2, children under 16 free. Foreign language guide may be requested. *DM*100

Wheelchairs: Free for visitors, available at the mainland entrance, lake entrance, and at the train station Schwedenschenke on the island.

Gardening questions and advice: Can be obtained in person or by telephone (07531/33191) from the Gardening Information Office in the Torbogengebaeude.

Events: From March to December there are scheduled monthly exhibits or conferences taking place on Mainau. Ask any German National Tourist Office for the year's calendar (Veranstaltungskalender).

A Great Gardener for Mankind

HERRENHAUSEN, SECRET ROSE GARDEN
Photo: Dorothy Loa McFadden, APSA

THE GARDEN IN COLOR ON PAGE 106

Chapter 9

Herrenhausen
Hannover, Germany

SOPHIE, ELECTRESS OF
HANNOVER

*A Glorious
Garden for the Arts*

eet me under the horse's tail" is what you
might say to your pretty blonde girl friend if
you lived in Hannover, Germany. (This is the
German spelling of the city's name.) The tail referred to
is that of the equestrian statue in the center of Ernst
August Platz, opposite the main railroad station. Riding
on this horse is Ernst August, first elector (ruler) of the
region of Hannover.

Archduke Frederic I of the Pfalz went to England at
age 16. He brought home as his bride Sophia Dorothea,
granddaughter of King James I of England. Their fifteen
children were brought up as if they were truly princes
and princesses, at first in Leiden, Holland, later in Germany. Sophie was the twelfth child, the fifth daughter.
She eventually married Ernst August who became the
first elector of Hannover.

Sophie had a very happy disposition. Throughout her

long life and its many sad events, her constant optimism and merry outlook was an inspiration to all those around her. She would say "You only live once, so why get upset over mishaps?" Yet she had a brilliant mind and enjoyed talking or corresponding with many intellectual people. Her mentor and close friend from her early youth on was the eminent German philosopher, historian, mathematician and physicist, Gottfried Leibniz. He was always amazed at her comprehension of the most difficult ideas he could present. Their discussions were in three fields: her family including every most distant member; politics and the recurrent European wars; and questions of a spiritual nature, religion. Together they tried very hard to promote a fusion of Protestants and Catholics in Europe, but without success.

Her oldest sister, Elizabeth, was considered to have one of the finest minds in Europe at that time, but her interests were entirely philosophical and religious, and in learning more languages.

When she became the wife of the elector of Hannover, Sophie stayed near him as much as possible. They made a trip to Italy in 1672, staying there for a year. This experience had quite an influence on Sophie's later life. They built a home there and created a garden which was designed by Martin Charbonnier, a Frenchman and pupil of Le Nôtre's. When they returned and began to live in a new palace in Hannover, Sophie soon became involved in creating vast gardens there.

The gardens of Herrenhausen had already been started in 1666, but it was Sophie who enlarged them from 1696–1714 and gave them new beauty, expanding them from the original 30 acres to finally cover 150 acres. She had the gardens designed by Martin Charbonnier, combining Italian, Dutch and French influences. They could accommodate hundreds of people and Sophie particularly enjoyed the masquerades there at carnival time during Lent.

She was very interested in drama, music and ballet and planned the outdoor theatre in the gardens, with gilded statues lining both sides of the stage. Here her own children often took part in a play or ballet. Today there are still many performances by international artists in this theatre from spring to fall, with plays by the likes of Moliere or Shakespeare.

Near this open air theatre there were long beds of tiny scroll work hedges filled in with thousands of small flowers, 263,000 pansies, for example. Today these have been replaced by colorful marble chips, as the bombings of World War II did much damage, and the city government which now owns the gardens could not afford such lavish expenditures. But the lovely designs remain, like the "chessboard" dotted with potted orange trees, and the many statues, pools and fountains, one sending its sprays up some 265 feet into the air, the tallest in Europe.

We can also still enjoy the charming "secret gardens" which Sophie planned, enclosed by high hedges which are now centuries old. There is a rose garden with a white lattice gazebo in each corner; an "Island Garden" featuring the tropical agapanthus or

HERRENHAUSEN OUDOOR THEATER
Photo by German National tourist Office

Lily of the Nile; and a miniature topiary garden where the small shrubs have been clipped into the forms of rabbits, squirrels and hens sitting among colorful flower carpets. Another "Secret Garden" is filled with a fine example of the colorful Knot Garden.

There are also fine performances of operas and excellent concerts offered in the Gallery, the building which was formerly the home of Sophie's family. Later, however, it held a most important place in her life, for in these exquisitely decorated rooms she held her "salons," discussions among the great intellectuals of Europe. Sophie also kept in touch with developments in England, knowing that as her brothers and sisters died, she was ever closer to

AN OPERA PERFORMANCE IN THE GALLERY BUILDING, 1964
German National Tourist Office

becoming England's next queen. But she could not understand the antagonism of the two parties there, based on their religious beliefs.

Unfortunately Sophie died just two months before the death of Queen Anne. She succumbed to a heart attack while she was taking her favorite morning walk in the gardens of Herrenhausen. So instead of Sophie, her son George became King George I of England. He had no interest in this change in his life. He had been brought up

DRAMA IN THE GARDEN

as a soldier, and was a totally unimaginative, stolid person who spoke no English. He continued to live in Hannover. He had divorced his wife and imprisoned her for life for a misdemeanor which was never satisfactorily proved. In the historical booklets about Britain's Kings and Queens published in England, the notes about him end with the words "the king died finally of apoplexy in Hannover, not very greatly regretted by his subjects."

His mother Sophie, however, will remain in all our memories as a great woman, whose creation and devotion to the splendid gardens of Herrenhausen have lived on for over 300 years. These gardens have always been open to the public, but being the property originally of the rulers, there were certain rules laid down for the "commoners." They are inscribed on a stone tablet still to be found near one of the closed gates. They caution (in German) that under threat of punishment, people "must not damage anything in the gardens... nor throw food to the swans... nor catch or even disturb the nightingales. They must sit on benches only if unoccupied by persons of higher rank... and obey orders of the watchman... and they *must not take any of their sins into the gardens with them.*"

Tips for Travelers

Location: In the city of Hannover. Can be reached easily by trolley, bus or taxi .

Events: The large commercial fairs of Hannover are well known, drawing businessmen from the entire world. For information about both commercial fairs in Hannover, and theater and music in Herrenhausen, contact: Hannover Fairs U.S.A. Inc., P.O.Box 7066, 103 Carnegie Center, Princeton, New Jersey 08540 U.S.A. Or in Hannover, Phone: 609-1202. Telex: 5101011751. Fax: (609) 9870092.

HELLBRUNN, BANQUET TABLE WITH WATER JOKES
Photo by Austrian Tourist Office

THE GARDEN IN COLOR ON PAGE 107

Chapter 10
Salzburg and Hellbrunn
Austria

ARCHBISHOP WOLF DIETRICH VON RAITENAU

Two Gardens for Three Mistresses

Two delightful gardens we can see in Salzburg today were created originally in the 16th and 17th centuries by the tremendously wealthy prince-archbishops who were both the civil and religious rulers of the city. Up to that time, such officials had busied themselves only with hunting and spending the riches pouring from the nearby gold and salt mines. They were not interested in improving the appearance or the living conditions for the inhabitants. But in 1587 a new epoch began for Salzburg.

This was when Wolf Dietrich von Raitenau, a descendant of the Medicis, became the city's new prince-archbishop. There is a charming contemporary account of his triumphal reception in Salzburg, riding at the head of a long procession of bishops and prelates, dukes and other nobles. All were decked out in their gayest satins, velvets and plumes, but they, like the citizens

75

lining the streets to watch, became soaked to the skin by the usual gentle Salzburg drizzle.

Wolf Dietrich, then only in his twenties, had grown up in Italy. He was steeped in Italian culture, the glories of its Renaissance architecture and art. His reaction to his first glimpse of this city of small hovels and squalid houses, of dark narrow streets breeding pestilence, was that it was barbaric, that he would change everything to make it as beautiful as his beloved Italy, a "Rome of the North."

He set about this with ruthless enthusiasm and energy. When, soon after his arrival, the cathedral caught fire, there were many townsfolk who murmured that he had either set it ablaze himself, or at least had done nothing to prevent the destruction that resulted. In the succeeding years he began what became, long after his time, the complete rebuilding of the great church, using St. Peter's in Rome as his model. He razed over 100 houses to make room for the lovely squares and streets we see surrounding the cathedral today and destroyed much of the old structure, including its statues and even the graves, to the horror of the citizens. A visitor to Salzburg today will find his coat of arms not only on the archbishop's palace, but also on the monastery of the Kapuzinerberg, the princely stables, the chapel of the church of St. Sebastian, the Franziskanerkirche and much more, all built during his reign.

For his mistress, the beautiful Salome Alt and her eleven children, he built the Palace which he called Altenau, a country retreat then outside the city walls. Next to this building (later renamed, as we shall see, the "Mirabell Palace,") are the remains of a once fabulous and extensive formal garden. Today the lovely "flower embroidery" beds in their Renaissance design give only a hint of the splendid expanse for outdoor entertaining which was planted in Wolf Dietrich's time. It is said that he designed some of the flowerbeds himself,

More definitely handed down to us from his reign is the enchanting "Dwarf's Garden." In the shade of ancient beech trees, tucked into alcoves of greenery, are the strange granite portraits of twelve dwarfs whom Wolf Dietrich had received as a gift from the Landgrave of Goettweig. Each was a gifted musician, dancer or mimic and as one studies the grotesque figures one can imagine their master's pleasure in their antics. Wolf Dietrich was an elegant man of the world. Though some portraits show him as a stern, ruthless ruler, there is another more human likeness in which his eyes sparkle and his bishop's beret is cocked roguishly over one ear. His was a flamboyant, lively and creative period. He changed Salzburg into the splendid Renaissance and early Baroque city which we see today.

Unfortunately the reign of this prince-archbishop came to a sad end. Wolf Dietrich had been feuding with the Elector of Bavaria for some time, when suddenly he decided to capture Berchtesgaden from his enemy. In retaliation, the duke managed to obtain the surrender of Wolf Dietrich's border city of Tettmoning, whereupon the prince succumbed to panic and fled with Salome Alt and much of his treasure to the south. There he was captured by the Bavarians and brought back to Salzburg for long and complicated hearings. In the end he was promised a ducal pension and his freedom, but neither was given to him. Instead, he was imprisoned in the grim fortress of Hohensalzburg in solitary confinement, without writing materials or visitors. He died there five years later among the rats and vermin. His beloved Salome Alt, meanwhile, had been exiled to the city of Wels.

Wolf Dietrich's successor as ruler of Salzburg was his cousin Markus Sitticus. He too had been steeped in the

Italian tradition, but his contributions to the life and appearance of Salzburg were of a different order. He outdid Wolf Dietrich in one respect, for he kept two mistresses instead of one. There was Mirabella, for whom he renamed the Altenau Palace when he presented it to her; and Madam Mabon, whom he installed in a new castle he built at Hellbrunn. Markus Sitticus laid the foundation of Salzburg's present reputation as the great festival city of culture. He installed a baroque theater in his residential palace and brought many operas to his new outdoor stage at Hellbrunn, his favorite place for entertaining at lavish parties.

In his youth in Italy, Markus Sitticus had undoubtedly seen some of the "water jokes" being introduced in formal gardens all over Europe. It had become fashionable to have hidden water pipes constructed among the trees and shrubbery, through which sprays of water could be aimed suddenly at unsuspecting guests by simply pushing a button. He brought Italian workmen to Hellbrunn and had a most elaborate example of these "jokes" installed there.

As we walk in this garden today and the guides demonstrate some of these contrivances, we can perhaps imagine the place peopled instead by the guests of this archbishop-prince, arriving for the first time at the entrance in their carriages, dressed unsuspectingly in their best pastel brocades and velvets. Then as they walked about admiring the romantic statues, or peered into cold encrusted grottoes, they would suddenly be drenched by streams of water coming from spouts hidden in the greenery. We can almost hear the raucous laughter of their host, manipulating a valve himself, as he saw some favorite lady or detested enemy meander into the right position. There must have been a sigh of relief when the guests, having dried themselves as best they could, finally sat down around the stone table anticipating a fine banquet. But after the first course had been served and everyone was relaxing, all the guests on one bench suddenly rose in horror as streams of water came out from where they had been sitting.

History will certainly give him more credit for his bringing opera and concerts to their present important place in the Salzburg area rather than for his fondness of "water jokes."

Tips for Travelers- SALZBURG

Mirabell Palace: Most of this fine building is no longer open to visitors, as the mayor's office and city administration offices are now located there. But one may see the famous Cherub Staircase, and the Marble Room unless a wedding is taking place there. There are also classical concerts in the Marble Room all the year around. This is where Leopold Mozart used to give concerts with young Wolfgang and his sister Nannerl. Music by Mozart is of course featured in many of the programs in the palace, as well as in concerts in the Archbishops' Residence. Programs for the entire year may be obtained from travel agencies in the USA or in Salzburg.

Tips for Travelers- HELLBRUNN

Features: The Palace, Trick Fountains and Folklore Museum are open with conducted tours of 30-40 minutes (minimum of 5 people) from 9 A.M. to 4:30 P.M. in April, , from 9 A.M. to 5 P.M. May to September, and 9 A.M. to 4:30 P.M. in October except when there are special events going on. Evening tours in July and August are at 6,7,8 and 9 P.M.

Admission Fees: AS48. for adults daytime or evening, AS24 for children. Admission to orangery and pheasantry is free. Sound and Light Shows at the Hellbrunn Zoo from October to March, daily 9 A.M.-4 P.M., April to September 8:30A.M. -6 P.M., Admission for adults, AS40, children AS20. Conducted tours are by arrangement. The Folklore Museum ("Monatsschloesschen") is open Easter to October from 9A.M.-5 P.M. Admission for adults AS15, children AS10.

Operas and concerts: Ask a travel agent in the USA or Austria for detailed list.

Two Gardens for Three Mistresses

THE ALHAMBRA, PATIO OF THE ARRAYANES,
Photo by James L. McFadden

THE GARDEN IN COLOR ON PAGE 108

Chapter 11

The Alhambra
Granada, Spain

The Creation of a
Wise Moorish Conqueror

W e are indebted to our famous American author, Washington Irving, not only for a delightful description of the beautiful buildings and gardens of the Alhambra and the summer palace of Generalife, but also for his portrait of Alhamar, the Moorish conqueror who created them, and was at the same time an enlightened, socially conscious ruler of his domain.

After the Moors had conquered Spain, they allotted various sections of the country to those who had distinguished themselves in battle. The whole region around Granada became Alhamar's territory. From the research which Washington Irving did in various books and manuscripts which were offered to him by friends in the area, we learn of an amazing character.

Mohammed ben Alhamar was a well educated Moorish nobleman, born in 1195, who had distinguished himself in the Moors' battle to conquer Spain. He was awarded the territory around Granada as his domain. In 1238 he decided to turn an old castle in the city of Granada into a magnificent palace which we now know as the Alhambra. Since then, writers and poets throughout the world have tried to put into words its splendor, its magnificence, its opulence, its pure aesthetic beauty. The name Alhambra means "red tower" because it is built of red stone. But this does not do justice to the ivory-colored delicacy of its buildings, the exquisite courtyards of flowers and fountains.

When Alhamar added the summer palace of Generalife on a higher, cooler plateau he created still another exquisite series of buildings, surrounded by courtyards, pools and fountains, and flowers. The Muslims had a saying, "God gives to those he loves a means of living in Granada." Truly these two creations fostered by Alhamar are the gemstones of Granada.

This Moorish kingdom was 220 miles long, stretching inland at some points up to sixty miles east along the Mediterranean coast from just north of Gibraltar to the rich ports of Malaga and Almeria. Granada was the capitol of the Muslim kings. Protected from the interior by formidable mountain ranges, whose cascading streams provided water for a broad network of irrigation, it had red soil and luxurious green fields that abounded in cattle, fruits, sugar cane, olives and cereals. The delicate jewelry of Granada was famed, as were its silks.

In order to water all the garden areas and supply the many fountains in the Alhambra, Alhamar had pipes laid from distant mountain streams. These are still supplying the water for plants, pools and fountains in the Alhambra we see today, more than 700 years later!

Four of the original garden courts are still to be seen. The largest and most important is the Court of the

Myrtles. Its large green pool has hedges of myrtles and orange trees along its sides, and at each end a loggia with alabaster columns is reflected on its shining surface. Nearby is the official residence, including the Hall of Benediction under a cedar cupola. Next is the Ambassadors' Hall where many lavish receptions were held. The architecture of the buildings throughout is delicate, elegant, graceful, planned for leisurely, indolent enjoyment.

The adjacent Court of the Lions is probably the best known and most photographed example of Moorish

JARDINES DEL PORTAL
Photo by James L. McFadden

architecture. The twelve stone lions supporting the alabaster central fountain basin are crude in execution , probably because of Moorish religious scruples against creating likenesses. But they have a great air of solemnity. Radiating from the Lions Court are the private apartments of the harem. From these windows the ladies could look down through the latticed jalousies to watch the dances and entertainment in the hall below. In his treatment of the harem, Alhamar showed his consideration for the happiness of others, for he insisted that there should be no quarrels among them, that they must live in harmony together He considered his wives to be his friends and intelligent companions.

The Creation of a Wise Moorish Conqueror

He was an astute humanitarian. In Granada he built hospitals for the blind, homes for the aged, and nursing homes. He often visited them unexpectedly to be sure they were being administered well. He built schools and colleges, organized an efficient police force and effective courts of justice. He established butcheries and public ovens for the people. His citizens adored him.

He supervised the production of fine silk, wool, and gold. He made the most of his distant silver mines so that they could pay for his many improvements.

He must have been very interested in horticulture, for he imported many rare plants and flowers, and spent much time in the fine gardens he had created. They were not only beautiful, but created a perfumed atmosphere of roses, jasmine, and orange blossoms. He lived to an active age of 79.

Washington Irving had read everything he could about Spain and the Alhambra throughout his life, and learned to speak and read Spanish easily. He became so absorbed in the history of the Moors there that he decided to go to Spain in 1824, where he lived in the ruins of the Alhambra for four months, meanwhile reading old manuscripts made available to him by his friends. He said "it was like living in the Arabian Nights." He wanted to stay there forever. His book, *The Alhambra*, was published in 1832. (It is now available for tourists in all the bookstores and souvenir shops of Granada in English, French, German, and Spanish.)

Unfortunately, in a misguided effort to please American tourists, a room has now been furnished and named "the room where Washington Irving wrote the *Alhambra.*" It contains elegant chairs, a desk, and even a spinet! Apparently the designers never read the *Alhambra* or they would have known that Irving did *not* write the book there. In fact, he only published it three years after he left Spain. While living in the ruins of Alhambra, he was given a little furniture by the old woman who was the caretaker of the place. It is doubtful that he had more than a bed, perhaps a simple chair and small table. But while living there, he was researching old documents about Alhamar in the extensive libraries of friends in the area and making copious notes.

In 1829, he received letters telling him that the new American president, Andrew Jackson, had appointed him as a secretary in the U.S. legation in London. It made Washington Irving very unhappy to leave his beloved paradise. It had been heaven to live in the Alhambra, to breathe in the unforgettable scent of the boxwoods, to relish the flavor of ripe figs, to inhale the mysterious scent of many flowers, and hear the nightingales sing. He had been mesmerized, completely enchanted. He accepted the appointment with great reluctance.

Today we still enjoy his fascinating descriptions of this wonderful old world. Fortunately the Alhambra and Generalife palaces have survived wars and earthquakes. When the French occupied the area, they rebuilt and reconstructed many of the beautiful buildings which had fallen into ruins from age and neglect. They are still there today for thousands of tourists to enjoy, as they imagine themselves again in this living Arabian Nights' Dream.

Tips for Travelers

Open: From April to September, Mondays through Saturdays 9:30 A.M. to 8:30 P.M. Sundays 9:30 A.M. to 6 P.M. Also at night when floodlit, Wed.-Sat. 10 P.M. to midnight.

Admission: Free Sunday afternoons from 3 P.M. No backpacks or large bags, please!

Tourist information: Casa de los Tiros. Ground floor. Plaza del Padre Suarez, Phone 22 10 22.

Hotels: There are a great many. Hotel Washington Irving is the most luxurious, refurbished and updated.

Events: The International Festival of Music and Dance, one of the most important in Europe. It is held at the end of June and beginning of July. Concerts are staged in the Palace of Carlos V and ballets take place in open air theatres of the Moorish Palace and the Generalife Gardens. The Holy Week processions in Granada include many beautiful floats. There are also many delightful Moorish and Christian festivals in nearby towns of the province.

Nearby Gardens: Botanical Garden 2 Malaga St., phone 27 84 00. Plants from all over the world. *Sierra Nevada Alpine Garden* 30km from Granada next to the University Hostel.

Notes

About the Author

Dorothy Loa McFadden always loved gardens, especially flower gardens. She had her own little plot around her playhouse, when she was a child in Scarsdale, New York.

Throughout her long life (she is now 90 years old) she shared her enthusiasms by writing for newspapers and magazines. The McFaddens became interested in photography. They both took color slides of gardens in Europe every summer on Jim's business trips.

As they showed these pictures at home, they noticed that many in the audience would say,"Why, I was right near there last summer, but I didn't know about that garden!" So Dorothy decided there was a real need for a guidebook to gardens open to the public in Europe. In 1965 it was published by David McKay Company as *Touring the Gardens in Europe*, covering 840 gardens in 18 countries. Although it is now out of print, travelers are still happily using this book in 1992, making notes from their own cherished copies or one from a library.

Dorothy got involved in many other careers over the years, besides writing. The McFaddens had two children, (she now has six grandchildren and seven great-grandchildren) so her early careers all involved young people. When her children were small, she organized a non-profit organization, Junior Programs, Inc. It sent its operas, ballets, and plays by adult professionals to audiences of over 4 million children in 40 states. She experimented with children's TV programs and planned and supervised the *New York Times* Boys' and Girls' Book Fairs each fall for ten years. Dorothy thoroughly enjoyed the creative challenges of all these careers.

In 1973 the Photographic Society of America awarded Dorothy the title of Associate member (APSA) for her assistance in forming and servicing a new Photo Travel Division. She founded the La Jolla Phototravelers club which still meets every month throughout the year. Her writing drew her into the National League of American Pen Women. She is a past president of the La Jolla Chapter, and was selected as their "Woman of Achievement" in 1985. She has been a member of the San Diego County Christian Writers' Guild from its inception, hosting one of its Critique Groups.

Now she is planning her next book, which will be a light-hearted autobiography, emphasizing the many amusing adventures in her life,and the joy of plunging into new, unusual activities which use the creative part of the brain. She is sure that she was always under the guidance of God.

She is now living in a beautiful retirement home, Wesley Palms, in San Diego, California. For six years she led a class at Wesley Palms for writing episodes from their life stories to hand down to their children and grandchildren. Many of these were printed in the bi-monthly newsletter which Dorothy edited and produced for five years, until she resigned to give her time and energies to writing *Drama in the Garden.*

Her home is one of many cottages that nestle in forty acres expertly planted with unusual flowering trees, shrubs, and flowers. As she walks each day to the big dining room, she is grateful for every leaf and blossom she passes, a bit of God's heavenly garden on earth.

Bibliography

Hampton Court
King Henry VIII, by John Bowle, Dorset Press, 1964
Men & Gardens, by Nan Fairbrother, Knopf, 1956

Levens Hall
Collins Book of British Gardens, by George Plumptre, Collins, 1985
The Pleasure Garden, by Ann Scott-Jones & Osbert Lancaster, Century, 1977

Powerscourt
The Gardens of Ireland, by Patrick Bowe-Hutchinson, 1986

Cawdor Castle
Scottish Castles, by Nigel Tranter, Macdonald, 1982
Scotland, by Nigel Tranter, Penguin, 1978
Macbeth the King, by Nigel Tranter, Coronet Books, 1978
The Gardener's Scotland, by Dawn Macleod

Mainau
Gute Nacht, Kleiner Prinz, autobiography by Graf Lennart Bernadotte, (in German) Wilhelm Heyne Verlag, 1977
Gardening for the Sake of Man, pamphlet by Frank Siegried, Schwarz KG, Konstanz

Herrenhausen
Beautiful Gardens Around the World, by Peter Coats, Little Brown, 1985
Kurfuerstin Sophie von Hannover, by Matilde Kroop, (in German), August Lax, Hildesheim, 1969

Mirabell

The Garden, an Illustrated History, by Julia S. Berrall, Viking, 1966.
The Gardens of Europe, by Penelope Hobhouse & Patrick Taylor,
   Random House, 1990.

Alhambra

The Alhambra, by Washington Irving, Heritage Press, 1969. (Fascinating descriptions plus imaginary legends.)

Books containing data on many gardens in this book.

Beautiful Gardens Around the World, by Peter Coats, Little Brown,
   1985. (Very fine photographs. Includes Mainau and Alhambra.)
Reader's Digest Great Gardens, Exploring Britain, 1984. (Includes
   Hampton Court and Levens Hall.)
The Pleasure Garden, by Ann Scott-Jones & Osbert Lancaster, Cen-
   tury, 1977. (Vaux-le-Vicomte, Roseraie, Hampton Court, Levens
   Hall)
The Garden, an Illustrated History, by Julia S. Berrall, Viking, 1966.
   (Still the finest accurate resource, with many gorgeous illustra-
   tions. Includes Vaux-le-Vicomte, Bagatelle, Hampton Court un-
   der Henry VIII, Mirabell, and Alhambra.)
The Gardens of Europe, by Penelope Hobhouse & Patrick Taylor,
   Random House, 1990. (Describes 700 gardens open to the pub-
   lic. Includes all gardens in this book except Cawdor Castle.)

The Gardens in Color

CHAPTER 1
VAUX-LE-VICOMTE, MELUN, FRANCE

CHATEAU VAUX-LE-VICOMTE
Photo by Dorothy Loa McFadden, APSA

GARDEN, VAUX-LE-VICOMTE
Photo by Dorothy Loa McFadden, APSA

DRAMA IN THE GARDEN

BAGATELLE, IRIS GARDEN
Photo by Dorothy Loa McFadden, APSA

BAGATELLE, AMERICAN PILLAR ROSE
Photo by R.C. Balfour, MBE, DHM

CHAPTER 3
ROSERAIE, PARIS, FRANCE

AMERICAN PILLAR ROSE
Photo by R.C. Balfour, MBE, DHM

ROSERAIE
Photo by R.C. Balfour, MBE, DHM

DRAMA IN THE GARDEN

ELIZABETHAN KNOT GARDEN
Photo by Dorothy Loa McFadden, APSA

GARDEN WALL NICHE
Photo by Dorothy Loa McFadden, APSA

DRAWING ROOM
Photo by Lucy Sclater, ARPS

TOPIARY GARDEN
Photo by Lucy Sclater, ARPS

DRAMA IN THE GARDEN

CHAPTER 6
POWERS COURT, IRELAND

Photo by Dorothy Loa McFadden, APSA

Photo by Dorothy Loa McFadden, APSA

CHAPTER 7
CAWDOR CASTLE, SCOTLAND

Photo by Dorothy Loa McFadden, APSA

LUPINES
Photo by B. Holmes

DRAMA IN THE GARDEN

PEACOCK OF FLOWERS
Photo by Brown & Jeannette Palmer

DAHLIAS
Photo by Dorothy Loa McFadden, APSA

AGAPANTHUS GARDEN
Photo by Dorothy Loa McFadden, APSA

ORANGE TREES
Photo by Dorothy Loa McFadden, APSA

CHAPTER 10
SALZBURG AND HELLBRUNN, AUSTRIA

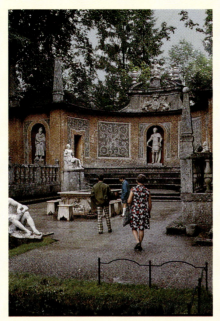

HELLBRUNN, GARDEN
Photo by Dorothy Loa McFadden, APSA

MIRABELL CASTLE, SALZBURG
Photo by Dorothy Loa McFadden, APSA

ABOVE, GENERALIFE,
JARDINES NUEVOS DEL TEATRO

RIGHT, ALHAMBRA,
JARDINES DEL PORTAL
Photos by James L. Mcfadden

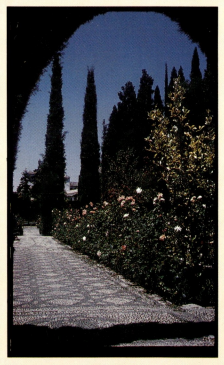